AF545246

A BLUE TONGUE

Pamphlet of Poems by Steve Levine

The Toothpaste Press West Branch, Iowa Summer, 1976

Some of these poems have appeared in *Brilliant Corners*, 432 *Review*, *Here It Is*, *In The Light*, *Out There*, *The Reader* (*Chicago*), *The Spirit That Moves Us*, *Telephone*, and *Victorious Photographs Broadsides*.

The Toothpaste Press West Branch, Iowa 52358

Library of Congress Cataloging in Publication Data
Levine, Steve, 1953—
A blue tongue.

I. Title
PS3562.E913B5 811'.5'4 76—41297
ISBN 0—915124—19—X

This project was partially funded by the National Endowment for the Arts, and endorsed by the Iowa State Arts Council.

CONTENTS

This book is dedicated to Arnold Aprill & Barbara Barg.

JUNE

wash my hands with Lava
feel nothing & be
primitive, proud
alternate
                    sit down then walk
hoe-down with a shoulder-holster
talk about nothing   itch
talk about invention
                                        iron pants
love the way you dry your hair
babble   stop
read Reverdy in the stifling heart

WOKE UP THIS MORNING

at the house
of Scott and Jean
"Turks take demi-tasse
for tea"
        Three
succeeding generations
    egg   Omelet   muenster
                of Ibrahim Pasha
did not possess a modicum
of the wealth, a spoonful of
such exquisite taste
                sugar
                brown sugar
                expertly
                pulverized
                beans
                for breakfast

THE CHAMBER I INHABIT IS FINALLY CLEARED

Beautiful weather
Just "beautiful"
"Just" the way you say "simply"

Is there a term, meaning a time
more beautiful? No. Doubt it.
Beautiful weather. Wonderment. Leaves like rust.

Wonderful crow fall in the yard making metal noisy
as they drift into the chain-link
fence. Blam! Beautiful ether.

I walked home and collapsed on the bed
I walked home
I walked home collapsed

On the bed, beautiful weather.
On the way home I heard a couple of heels scrapping
behind me. Beautiful wonderment of weather.

Along the concrete
I heard two heels scrapping.
I heard scraping, collapsing on the bed, behind me

I think it was the springs.
They, no doubt, are beautiful, touching, tired.
A persistent noise has followed me home.

Shit! this persistent noise has followed me home.
Crow metal beautiful link the scrape. Rust,
is there a term more beautiful?

AIR

The smoke
above
the barber opens his atelier
                floats
    false moustaches
under
        the beer company ad
among newspapers
and smiles
like the god of beriberi

VICTORIOUS PHOTOGRAPHS

1.

up at 11
slept 2 hrs.
approximately
passed the previous night's
intention, feeling alright
nonetheless

on this Nov. 12 first snow day
in Chicago
subtropical Tahiti
was an insane thing
to imagine, but I imagined it
was nice
when waking

Then, once walking
out of the house, walking

I saw:
a single lady break into Greenwood's
wrought iron fence God!
it was astounding it broke the fall

and blurting rabid Vladimir
his own beloved
Anna Blossom
nowhere
to be found

2.

Super M I am
Master of naive art
The goldfish twirl
In the coca–cola
Glass deep line breaks
In quick succession

Because of that unbeatable power
Imagination
I smoke
The dope from two pipes
Own a corkscrew
His name Alphonse
The second hand sweeps
5:47:50

When light goes out
Outside I say
"Come on in"
Should've said I just turned on
The livingroom lamp
To make it clear, then

A new national bestseller
By Gunter
"Local Anaesthetic" Grass
The Ancient Mason Civilization

Of Peru and *Tales*
By the man who changed
His name become apparent

But not me
Master of naive art
Free trips
Six couples
Columbia
Plus 200 Polaroids in red

3.
On Curious 57th

I stood straight and sharp, bore
a newly acquired volume, the works
of Vladimir Mayakovsky, quite aware
of the deliberate looks and
older eyes, tough
indignant lines, threatening
his face, his photograph, resisting
comparison

WAVERING EMOTION

At night, particularly
On a clear, cloudless night
Temperature often increases with height.
Now I can't get much higher, no
Clouds in my head. What
Would you say if I said I'm hot
Too? I'm filled, in fact
With the thought of that glowing
Wit & warmth, that is, your person. You
Personally, your personality, the clarification
I notice when images of wavering emotion
Get solid, gain form, and fill my day-
To-day life, become that light.
The light is this, more accurately
These thoughts. These thoughts
                    sparkling particles
            that appear and move

Onto the page. It's not my imagination!
I'm telling you the truth. I'll even shut the TV off
If you'll come over! Embodiment of Radiance
Hot shot, near nova, come up, I'm waiting, step on it!

MODERN SCIENCE

I put my heart on a wire
Tug it
Send it off
Chicago to California
It sees lots of wondrous sights
In the interval along the way

For instance, it sees the florescent flatlands
    of the bizarre but tastefully
    exotic Midwest, where
    chrome is grown.
It is astonished
By this marvel of Le Science Moderne

The Plains are truly plain in comparison

Though it, my heart, is not surprised
To see the exploding Indians
    of the Plains.
But now I think it's gone too far

My heart, going the wrong way
Get back here, muscle!

I unhook it, wrench it
Inside out, hook it up anew, and...
It goes on its groove back down the wire
Through high blue grey green
It can be seen heading southwest

My heart. It is real red
And pumping like a motherfucker!
But it's nothing like a cock.
It's a red heart
It's a red running heart
It's a red heart running out
    of Arizona.
I put it on a wire
Tugged it
To make sure
Sent it off.
From Chicago to California.
It's very big
To see you, and happy
After its trip and many exciting adventures

BABE RUTH

Bambino, the Babe,
as I knew him, the Sul
tan of Swat, an adventurer,
a great explorer, but a poet
and philosopher as well. His
incredible ability to hit home
runs was matched only by his huge
appetite for good living. Whatever
he did he did in a big way. He was
the first man to fly over the North
Pole, first man to fly over the South
Pole. He explored more unknown land
area than any man in history. "Man"
he said, "wants to know and when he ceases
searching for knowledge, he ceases to be
a man." He was one of the key figures
in the Romantic Movement. Children

loved him, fans flocked to see him
and a nation idolized him. He was
the symbol of a carefree happy day,
an age that made heroes and made Babe
Ruth stand head and shoulders above others

GIFT STARS

I

Baron Sphere
And the heavenly circus
See the narrow stitch

O look at him! He
Is what wit means
Beneath a tough lyrical grease

In and out in and out
With the subtlety
Of feet

She said
And meant it
With conviction

II

Behind her rapture
A philosophy:
We are so beautiful

But have to die
Someday
So I miffed her

In the dufus
And in no time
It had almost no effect

The sun got up
The trees came out
We end on a carefully Protestant note

III

What's the earthly flame?
What's the pure flame?
What's the use?

The flourishing wreath
Repays innocent action
Philocles, Pyrocles, Amphialus

And Gentle Joe stop't spitting
Lips congealed
With heat

Aurora! Goddess
Of dawn I can't help
But yawn in your presence

THINGS THAT EXCITE

Good eating, good drink
All sorts
Of mime, of music,
Spicer's *A Book*
of Music, mellifluous
Fields of humming blue
In general, the green
Expanse, this planet
I live on, Carol's
Broad flat ass, her slight
Excitement & reddening shock
To see her name, let alone
Her ass, in a manner
Of speaking, mentioned

C

Crazy & loud learned to blink
To view the sand & nod
Lazily bebaubled w/ stolen
Hazards, the stones
Of Caracas' depths

Say you, Master
Of China Talk, the Appalachian
Dobro, the Incomparable
Fucker—   Run
Banality away forever!

Here, do the job, 12 roses
And assorted scrolls
Will be my gift
To the non-greasiest
Colloidally perfectest you

For adoration
Simple   Strips
Wrapped   Amount   Tool
Tows all my stomachs by

Towards our pretty temporal
Most monumental desires
Immutable, C, almost
Like the weather

A BLUE TONGUE

Appearing to be behind her ears, 3
crocodile skin bags, but nothing else
besides a few bottles, a rum rug, a blue
tongue devouring blackberries

Not an atom of an interest
in the things: Hunt-balls,
spillikens, cats
quarreling and dispersed

In the hall   she was
a small woman, baggage
being loaded
                    lolling out
every marine original—

Mustn't forget those
marine originals, her
scruples or my extract. Sure
heavily triangular, piece of copper metal

Had the engine of the car, this car, that car
has no artistic tastes, or breeding, by
a curious retrogression, a blue tongue
devouring blackberries

"BLACK BAMBINO"
after Berrigan

intrudes without intent. Amen

Blaise

le grand fromage
the 3-way wedge

PRUDENCE ORGY

BABY WHALE Redimark
tips, & March

2. handsome handmade flickerbooks

"The Tabolets"

did the head (undefined) and Kiwi (tan)

Polish? from Pottstown, Pa.

on Mulac's desk 19464
in Mulac's room USA

Imagined this Iowa disordered

totally

GALORE, overall

Handset & printed by Jim Hanson; designed by Allan Kornblum. This first edition of 450 copies was printed with Plantin and Bulmer types on Strathmore Beau Brilliant paper, then handsewn into wrappers.